Kemet 101
An Introduction to Ancient Egyptian History and Culture

Perry Khepera Kyles

African Diaspora Press

"An African worldview for an African world experience"

www.adponline.info
713-900-5062

Other Books Published by African Diaspora Press

Classic Book Series
The Negro, by W.E.B. DuBois, 1915.
Stolen Legacy, by George G.M. James, 1954.
Wonderful Ethiopians of the Ancient Cushite Empire by Drusilla Dunjee Houston, 1926.
Walker's Appeal, by David Walker, 1830
Egyptian Ideas of the Future Life by E.A. Wallis Budge, 1899
The Kybalion, by The Three Initiates, 1908
The Egyptian Book of the Dead Translated by E.A. Wallis Budge, 1895
Ancient Egypt: Light of the World by Gerald Massey, 1907

Africana Studies Book Series
Egypt and Her Neighbors, edited by Michael Ogbeidi, 2011.
Violence in God's Name: Christian and Muslim Relations in Nigeria by Christian Van Gorder, 2012.

The African Diaspora Lecture Series (DVD)
The African Diaspora Lecture Series is a series of public lectures given by Dr. Perry Kyles at the Eunoch Pratt Free Library in Baltimore, MD. The series addresses the most important themes in African Diaspora History beginning with Humanity's African origins. This series utilizes a wide range of methodologies including archival materials, secondary sources, field research, genetics, and linguistics. Topics include:
1. The African Origin of Humanity.
2. The Foundations of Nile Valley Civilization.
3. Ancient Egypt in Global Context.

Published in Houston, Texas by African Diaspora Press
www.adponline.info
713-900-5062

Manufactured in the United States of America

ISBN 13:

Preface

Kemet 101 is designed to provide a balanced introduction to the ancient civilization known by its citizens as Kemet, commonly referred to as Ancient Egypt in recent times.

The conclusions drawn in this text emanate from a number of different sources, methodologies, and intellectual communities. The primary objective is to provide the reader with a proper historical, scientific, and spiritual foundation for understanding the Ancient Nile Valley civilizations.

Teachers of history, spirituality, geography, anthropology, archeology, etc. will find this book an excellent reference text.

Kemet 101 provides images of over fifty important maps, artifacts, and other relevant images.

Part 1, "The Foundations of Nile Valley Civilization", begins with the "up south" origin of Nile Valley culture and addresses several aspects of cultural evolution.

Part 2, "Ancient Egypt in Global Context", addresses the history of Ancient Egypt beginning with Pepi II, who ruled longer than any other monarch in human history, and concludes with the legacy of Ancient Egypt.

Succinct and clearly written, this text is appropriate for anyone seeking reliable information on the most influential cultures in human history.

Perry Khepera Kyles, Ph.D

Table of Contents

The Foundations of Nile Valley Civilization

The Two Cradle Theory contrasts the evolutionary paths of the Southern Cradle and the Northern Cradle.[1] These two different paths explain cultural differences as well as conflicting worldviews that are with us today. The Southern Cradle began in the heartland of Africa - in the Great Lakes region and the regions of contemporary Kenya and Tanzania. The Southern Cradle came to practice a sedentary way of life much earlier than the European population. This was enabled by early Africans' realization that they needed to work with nature. Thus, they strove to be in harmony with nature and in harmony with the universe. Their whole conceptualization of all life revolved around this concept and the high cultures of the Nile Valley emerged with this worldview as its guiding principle.

The *Shemsu Heru* migrated throughout the tropics spreading this original human culture.[2] That original human culture flourished and from it Ta Seti, located in Contemporary Sudan, became the world's first nation-state. Further downstream the nation of

---

[1] The Two Cradle Theory was named by the great Senegalese scholar Cheikh Ante Diop. Read his *Civilization and Barbarism* for an in-depth treatment of the theory.

[2] The literal translation of Shemsu Heru is "followers of Heru". They are recognized as the people who migrated out of Ethiopia and brought "high culture" to the land that became Kemet or Ancient Egypt. For more information see Charles S. Finch III, M.D., *The Star of Deep Beginnings: The Genesis of African Science and Technology*, (Decatur: Khenti Inc.), 1998, pg. 34.

Kemet emerged and became the greatest country in human history. These African civilizations of the Nile Valley emerged as matrilineal societies - meaning that the female bloodline was central to succession rights and other matters of lineage. Also the female played a major role in agriculture, which provided sustenance for the people. This contrasted with the Northern Cradle, from which the Asian and European ways of life emerged. Due to the harshness of the environment in the Northern cradle the developmental path was different. Thus these communities came to exhibit innate insecurities. They also exemplified a greater inclination toward aggressiveness, a greater inclination toward violence, and a diminished appreciation for womanhood. In these nomadic populations females were burdensome since they cannot fight or hunt as fiercely, yet required vital resources such as food. The contrast between the two cradles explains the evolution of humanity and the historical developments that have taken place since these cultural divergences began to unfold. It may be best to chart the beginning of this great divergence about 100,000 ya (years ago), which is when human beings migrated away from continental Africa to less hospitable regions of the Earth.

The Two Cradle Theory in Antiquity

The Two Cradle Theory provides a comprehensive human evolutionary history. The concept is a rather old one that got somewhat lost over recent millennia. For example, an ancient literary document called *The Instruction of Merikare* (circa. 3000 B.C.E), which was written 5000 years ago, reveals that the Ancient

Egyptians would have taken Diop's theory as a matter of fact:

> Lo the miserable Asiatic he is wretched because of the place he's in short of water, bare of wood, its paths are many and painful because of mountains, he does not dwell in one place, food propels his legs he fights since the time of Horus.[3]

The author of this primary source is expressing that environmental factors led to the cultural divergence that created the Northern cradle. Thus, at this point in history Ancient Egyptians clearly understood why the Asiatics' culture developed in the way that it did.

European scholars of Antiquity also came to this same realization. Pliny, a Roman scholar of the 1st century C.E., stated:

> For it is beyond question that the Ethiopians are burnt by the head of the heavenly body near them, and are born with a scorched appearance, with curly beard and hair, and that in the opposite region of the world the races have white frosty skins with yellow hair that hangs straight; while the latter are fierce owing to the rigidity of their climate but the former are wise owing to the mobility of theirs.[4]

---

[3] Jacob Carruthers, *Essays in Ancient Egyptian Studies*, (Los Angeles: University of Sankore Press), 1984, pg. 18.
[4] Robin Walker, *When We Ruled: The Ancient and Medieval History of Black Civilizations*, (United Kingdom: Every Generation Media), 2006, pg. 104.

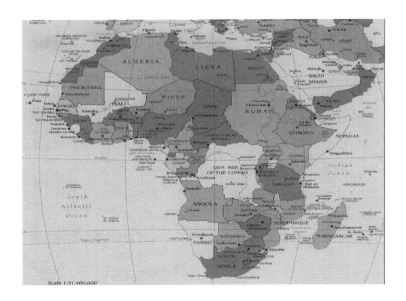

Contemporary Map of Africa

To fully understand the relationship between environment and the evolution of ancient Nile Valley culture as Pliny expressed above, it is necessary to know some geography of the region. The Nile River is the longest river in the world flowing 4,100 miles. The Nile River, or Hapi as the Ancient Egyptians referred to it, flows from its origin in the heartland of Africa northward and ultimately empties into the Mediterranean. It is important to know Khartoum, which is where the White Nile and the Blue Nile come together. In antiquity rich soil called silt flowed within the current of the Nile. The depositing of this rich soil along the river is what made this land fertile on each bank of the Nile. Most of the water that flows into the Sudan and Egypt comes from the highlands of Ethiopia.

The "Up South" Origin of Nile Valley Culture and Technology

The power of integrated knowledge gave our human ancestors great creativity and problem solving capabilities. As you would expect, they found in nature the tools to advance their technological needs and aesthetic tastes. One example is the mining of hematite in Swaziland. Iron is created by separating the hematite from iron ore. According to carbon dating, these mines are dated to be 43,000 y.a. [5] The conventional wisdom says that iron smelting began outside of Africa 1600 B.C.E., however we know for a fact that iron smelting existed in Kenya 2600 B.C.E. [6] Therefore the developmental process, obviously began in the southern stretches of Africa. There was no mining for manganese or flint anywhere outside of Africa until 8000 B.C.E. so technologically speaking, the Africans in the South were the first to establish this whole developmental path toward iron smelting that eventually developed in various places throughout the world.

The Ishango Bone (above)

Another important anthropological finding with implications for the origin of human civilization in Africa is the Ishango Bone, which is dated to be about

---

[5] Charles Finch, *Star of Deep Beginnings*, pg. 26.
[6] Ibid., pg. 27.

25,000 years old. It was found on the western bank of the Nile, in the Democratic Republic of Congo. The exact usage of the Ishango Bone has been disputed but there are two propositions. The first is that the Ishango bone was used as a calculator – a conclusion drawn from the belief that the notches on the bone represent systematized calculations. The other is that it is associated with the lunar cycle. The greater significance of the Ishango Bone is that it illustrates the existence of abstract thought and the expression of abstract thought in writing.

European writers of antiquity were well aware of the preeminence of Africa in human history and looked to Africa for their spiritual and intellectual roots. Homer's *The Iliad* circa 850 B.C. is the first piece of European literature ever written. In *The Iliad* Homer wrote: "…Zeus had yesterday to Ocean's bounds set forth to feast with Ethiop's [Ethiopia's] faultless men and he was followed there by all the gods." Homer insinuates preeminence of Ethiopian civilization and culture in Antiquity.

Consistently, along with genetic and linguistic evidence, European writers of Antiquity corroborate the conclusions of Drusilla Dunjee Houston and other Afrocentric scholars - that the indigenous Africans of the heartland are the forefathers and foremothers of the Ancient Egyptians. One Greek scholar of Antiquity by the name of Diodorus Siculus wrote: "They say also that the Egyptians are colonists sent out by the Ethiopians, Osiris [Ausar] having been the leader of the colony." He continued:

For, speaking generally, what is now Egypt, they

maintain, was not land but sea when in the beginning the universe was being formed; afterwards, however, as the Nile during the times of its inundation carried down the mud from Ethiopia, land was gradually built up from the deposit.[7]

He then commented on the diffusion of culture down the Nile:

For instance, the belief that their kings are gods, the very special attention which they pay to their burials, and many other matters of a similar nature are Ethiopian practices, while the shapes of their statues and the forms of their letters are Ethiopian.[8]

Here Diodorus is advancing the realization that the divine kingship concept and the Kemetic language have an Ethiopian origin.

The Rise of Nation States in the Nile Valley: Ta Seti and Kemet

To fully understand Kemetic (Ancient Egyptian) history, it is important to understand the periodization of the different historical eras. The idea of Kemet having an Old Kingdom, a First Intermediate Period, a Middle Kingdom, a Second Intermediate Period, and a New Kingdom were borrowed from a Kemetic priest named Manetho, wrote in the 3rd century B.C.E. The

---

[7] Robin Walker, *When We Ruled*, pg. 105
[8] Diodorus Siculus, *Book III*.

term "dynasty" refers to a particular lineage of kings. If that particular line of kings changed then a new dynasty began. As the name suggests, the Old Kingdom was the oldest and earliest dynasties of Kemet. The Middle Kingdom was the time period between the First and Second intermediate periods. What the intermediate periods signify are periods of great instability. The New Kingdom was the last sequence of Kemetic dynasties.

Ta Seti, which means "Land of the Bow", was the first monarchy in human history. It was established in the vicinity of Qustul and had a great cultural influence on Kemet. One of these influences is the concept of divine kingship, which means that the Pharaoh is thought of as divine representative of god on Earth - he is thus "Heru on Earth". The representation of the king as a hawk also has a Nubian origin and the best evidence for this was found in a cemetery Nubia in 1964 by Kenneth Seal. This cemetery is underwater today because of the building of the Aswan dam that was finished in 1970, however the evidence supports the conclusion of an "up south" origin of Kemetic civilization (see the following images). At some point upper Kemet was able to physically overtake Nubia. The first thing they did was establish their independence from Nubia. What enabled them to do so? In some places, downstream from that 6th Cataract (which the Europeans refer to as the first cataract) the Nile overflowed prior to the establishment of the Aswan Dam. That overflow was used to build canals and such to ensure that not only were villages spared from flood, but provided water to be used for land irrigation. Coming into that knowledge and

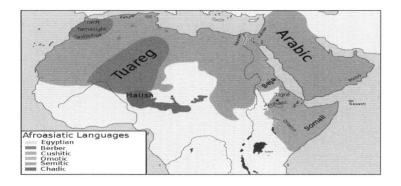

Ethiopic/Afroasiatic Language Map

The map of African language families enables the use of linguistic findings, which is a very fruitful methodology. The linguistic evidence illustrates the centrality of Africa, Ethiopia specifically, in human linguistic development. As we trace back humans' origins by looking at their genes, we can trace back cultural origins simply by tracing their linguistic origins. One of the largest of the African linguistic families is the Ethiopic family - what European scholars call Afro-Asiatic languages. Arabic, which they call a Semitic language, is spoken throughout northern Africa – a consequence of Arab colonization. Hausa, in Northern Nigeria, and various other ethnic groups over to the east are included in the "Afro-Asiatic" group. All of these languages have one origin. That origin is in Ethiopia, which is also the place where the oldest homo sapien fossils are found. Since the whole of this language family originated in Ethiopia, there is no reason for this language family to be called "Afro-Asiatic". The whole linguistic group should be referred to as Ethiopic.

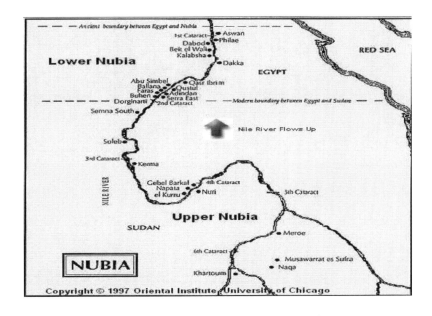

Map of Nubia

Nubia means "land of gold". The map shows Nubia as it was well into the New Kingdom. Take a look at the cataracts including the 6th, 5th, 4th cataract on down to the 1st cataract. The river is flowing down stream and the land is much higher in the southern parts. The river's stream and the diffusion of culture both flow down the Nile River – thus it is senseless to refer to the southernmost cataract as the 6th cataract and the northernmost as the 1st cataract. Therefore to the southernmost cataract is the 1st cataract and the northernmost is the 6th cataract. Also, it is important to note the presence of Qustul. In antiquity Qustul was in Nubia and not Egypt. Still today some of the Nubian symbols that would be used by Kemetic people later on are still present in carvings.

Image of an Ankh in Ancient Nubia Region of Contemporary Egypt

The ankh has pre-Kemetic origins-meaning that it existed before there was a Kemet and before the two lands united to create Kemet. The ankh symbolizes harmony. Simply put, the loop at the top of the ankh represents a womb and the straight part at the bottom symbolizes the phallus. This does not represent a simplistic reference to sexual union. What it depicts is the Kemites conceptualization of the world. Thus it would be safe to say that ankh is a metaphor for harmony that originated upstream from Kemet.

Excavated Nubian Burial

Nubian burials that were excavated tell us a lot about the Nubian way of life. Here the deceased was buried with both bracelets and pottery. The bracelets could mean a couple of different things - they could mean trade was common or that this person that accumulated wealth. Pottery signifies sedentary life that was enabled by agriculture. The foundation of these sophisticated civilizations was agriculture, which enabled them to meet their basic needs without moving.

understanding enabled them to sustain a much larger population. Greater agricultural yields enabled greater population density. The way that they were able to sustain this particular structure is that about 90% of the population was farmers and they paid taxes in grain.

Another important issue in the ascendancy of Kemet is the issue of leadership. You probably hear a lot about Narmer or Menes, and the Aha that came after Narmer. The greatest Kemetologist of all time, or at least one of the best, is Dr. Yosef Ben Jochannan. Dr. Ben has expressed a belief that there were three Aha kings, including an Aha king who was before the person we refer to as Narmer. In Upper Egypt there was a tradition of powerful kings developing and they were able to organize the people to take advantage of this population growth. Eventually they liberated themselves from the people up stream (Ta Seti) who had a much smaller population. I believe that there was a weakness in leadership in Nubia. During this time period Narmer united Upper and Lower Kemet. This union came to be used metaphorically as well. Narmer also established the city of Menefer, which is today referred to as Memphis. He consolidated his power by marrying into a royal family from Lower Kemet.[9]

---

[9] For a wonderful, brief biography of Narmer see pg. 3 of Ashra and Merira Kwesi's *Afrikan Builders of Civilization: A Pictorial History of Famous Personalities from Ancient Egypt* (Kemet Nu Productions, 1995).

Artifact/Incense Burner from Qustul Excavation

Above is an incense burner that was found at Qustul. It has several images that provides insight into the world of Ta Seti. The incense burner possesses images of a serekh, which is a symbol for kingship that was later borrowed by Kemites. You can also see a bound captive and the crown that would later be used as the crown of Upper Egypt. The beard is apparent and so is a flail. You see Ausar (Osiris) holding the flail and you also see him holding the crook. Thus the incense burner serves as corroborating evidence for Diodorus claim that I presented earlier in this essay. The hawk standing atop the castle is a symbol of kingship.

FIGURE 5

GEBEL SHEIKH SULEIMAN

Above is from one of the Nubian monuments. Apparently there is a hawk atop a castle, a bound captive who is bound with the symbol for Ta Seti "Land of the Bow", and also Ta Seti routing their rivals. In some of these images the rival of Ta Seti is the actual land that became Upper Egypt.[10]

---

[10] For more archeological evidence support this conclusion see pgs. 94-98 of Bruce Williams' "The Lost Pharoahs of Nubia" in Ivan Van Sertima, *Egypt Revisited*, (New Brunswick: Transaction Publishers), 2006 (first published 1989). Jacob Carruthers' *Essays in Ancient Egyptian Studies*, pgs. 21-24 was very helpful in deciphering the meaning of the symbols on Nubian artifacts.

How and Why Were the Egyptian Pyramids Built?

There are two popular theories as to how the Ancient Egyptians built pyramids. One theory is that they were built with ramps - the other is that they were built with levers. If you go to various ancient monuments throughout contemporary Egypt you will see ramps at temples that were built with very large stones. That is one reason to argue that they might have built these pyramids with ramps. Also, they erected the Tehkenu with ramps, so there is some evidence that suggests that maybe they did build them with ramps.[11] However, there are scholars who believe that building these ramps would have taken as much effort as it took to build the pyramids and that they were built with levers, or as Herodotus says "machines". I think that it was unlikely that they built them with levers - I think it was a lot of toil, experience, know how, and a lot of trial and error. That knowledge was passed down over centuries and enabled them to erect the sequence of smooth pyramids that they built.

Why were the Egyptian pyramids built? In some cases they were tombs. For example, Imhotep's step pyramid was a tomb for King Djoser. In other cases they were symbolic with the body being buried in Upper Kemet. It is believed that the bodies of the royal Kemites whom the cenotaphs honored were buried in Upper Kemet.[12] There have been several propositions as to what the pyramids symbolized. One theory is that they symbolize sun rays, another is that they represent

---

[11] A tehken (tehkenu for plural) are spiritual constructions that often stood outside of temples. Europeans refer to tehkenu as "obelisks".
[12] A cenotaph is an empty tomb.

(above) Dr. Kyles at Nilometer in Philae.
(below)Nilometer at Aswan.

The Nile overflows annually and the extent to which it overflows determines the amount of taxation for that particular year. These nilometers are in Philae and Aswan respectively. Notches along the nilometer were used to measure the amount of water and thusly determined the amount of taxation in grain for that year.

The Narmer Palette

Much of what we know about Narmer comes from an
artifact called the Narmer Palette. Here Narmer is
presented wearing the hedjet, the crown of Upper
Kemet. On one side of the palate Narmer is depicted
wielding a mace, which is basically a stick with a rock on
the end. He is about to smite an Asiatic enemy. These
rivals are the populations that are coming over from the
Middle East area by way of the Sinai over into Africa.
How do we know who they are? The symbols denote
the marshlands of the region from which the Asiatics
emerged. The lower level of the palate illustrates the
rivals that have already been vanquished. On the other
side Narmer is wearing the crown of Lower Kemet. In
various places on the palette you see the bull, which
symbolizes the vitality of the Pharaoh. Thus the
Narmer Palette and other sources like Manetho, reveal
to us that it was Narmer who united Upper and Lower
Kemet.

In the Old Kingdom emerged the great master teacher Imhotep. The image above is a sculpture of Imhotep that is in the Metropolitan Museum in New York City. This scroll in his hand symbolizes abstract thought.

This structure was designed by Imhotep and is referred to as the Mastaba pyramid, or the step pyramid. The pyramids built after the mastaba pyramid built upon Imhotep's design.

Above Imhotep is depicted as a deity. He was from a town called Ankhtaui (which means "life of the two lands") that was near Memphis. What Imhotep is best known for is his success as a physician. He is believed to have healed thousands of people and taught the profession to several others.[13]

---

[13] For an excellent, well-researched biography of Imhotep see pgs. 71-91 of Charles S. Finch's *The African Background to Medical Science: Essays on African History, Science and Civilization*, (London: Karnak House), 1990.

On the heels of Imhotep's mastaba pyramid architects attempted to build pyramids with the exact same dimensions on each side, all coming to a single point. During the 4th Dynasty a pyramid was built for King Neb Ma'at Sneferu. The pyramid changes angles about halfway through. This was not a decision made by the architect – it was a decision made well into the building of it. Once design flaws were realized this adjustment were made to quickly complete the project.

The second attempt by Sneferu's architects was successful. This pyramid is 343 feet high and has over two million stones. The interior stones are about 50,000 lbs. The stones on the outer casing vary in size but generally weigh much less than the inner stones.

This is the Ghiza Plateau. On the far left is the Great Pyramid. When that pyramid was built for King Khufu it appeared to be higher. The tradition of pyramid building was big in the 4th dynasty. You see a pyramid built by Khufu's son Khafre - it looks bigger than Khufu's but it is built on higher ground. The Third pyramid from the left was built for Menkara who was the grandson of Khufu. Khufu, Khafre, and Menkara are grandfather, son and grandson. Menkara's pyramid is about 281 ft. high.

Recent studies based on field research shows that the pyramids of Kemet (Ancient Egypt) were built by paid laborers that were also Egyptian. One of the early Jewish writers by the name of Josephus attempted to prove the antiquity of the Jews by claiming that Jewish slaves built the Egyptian pyramids of mud and straw. Clearly they were made of stone.

(Above) Naturally occurring rock structures in the region of Upper Kemet/Nubia/Contemporary Egypt. Note the pyramidal shape.

I believe that these pyramids symbolized the primeval mound, the mound from which life sprang forth and/or their people originated. In Nubia I saw mountainous rocks that look pyramidal in form (see image above). The water in the above image would have been much lower before the building of the Aswan dam – this would likely give a greater pyramidal effect. I strongly believe that the physical environment of this sacred region of Upper Kemet had an architectural influence on the establishment of the pyramids in Kemet.

the primeval mound of their origins. Another is that they were portals of sorts to the next realm of existence. I believe that there is significance credence to the latter two propositions and the answer would be a combination of these two. I believe this do to the reverence in which Kemites showed to the highland areas such as Abydos and the pyramidal shaped natural rock constructions in Nubia.

What Made the Kemites Successful State Builders?

From a technological, spiritual, and cultural standpoint no civilization has surpassed what the Kemites were able to achieve. Foremost they formed a very stable – meaning that they were able to provide for themselves sustenance, shelter, and safety. They had group cohesion, not simply from the perspective of family but from the perspective of community and society. They had a common goal, common leadership, and a common spiritual concept that guided them. It did not matter which historical epoch or which creation story was most common in your nome, they all believed in divine order, which they called *MA'AT*.[14]

Another important aspect is that they were able to keep foreigners at bay. It is no coincidence that Kemet's intermediate periods were resulted from the presence of foreigners.[15] Foreigners came in and had a destructive effect on the stability of those societies. Also, they were highly spiritual people who saw

---

[14] A Kemetic "nome" was a political designation given to various regions of the country.
[15] This topic is one of the main themes of the following chapter.

divinity in all life. The Kemite spiritual outlook supported what we would today call "free will" and certainly would have scoffed at the notion of a human being "born in sin". This "born in sin" concept is consistent with the pessimistic nature of European cosmology.

Kemetic Perspectives on Human Creation

Among the oldest human creation stories ever known to humanity is the Memphite Theology. It is believed to have originated in the city of Memphis, Egypt (called Menefer by the Kemites). Ptah is the name of the Creator/God in the Memphite Theology. In this conceptualization Ptah also had a consort – she was a deity by the name of Sehkmet. There are many colorful stories related to the deity of Sehkmet. If you ever go to Metropolitan or Brooklyn Museum in New York City you will see several statues of Sekhmet. According to Kemetic mythology Sekhmet was far from a damsel in distress - if you crossed Sekhmet, or practiced unethical behavior, you had a heavy price to pay. As with the Ankh, the fact that Kemites thought to depict the masculinized Creator as having a feminine complement says much of their world view. Far from the misogynistic world view that originated in the Northern Cradle, the Kemetic world view recognized the divinity of men and women, and also acknowledged the necessity of unity between them to create wholeness. They were not polar opposites but two distinct parts creating one whole – both biologically and metaphorically. In the Memphite Theology the Creator created four pairs of *Neteru*. Neteru are deities that can be thought of as aspects of the divine that exists within humanity – male and female.[16] The first pair of Neteru was Nun and Nunet. Nun symbolized the primeval waters while his female consort, Nunet, symbolized formed matter. Huh and Huhet - boundlessness and boundedness. Kuk and Kuket - darkness and light. Amen and Amenet –that which is hidden and that which is manifest.

The most important mythological story in human history is the Ausarian Resurrection – sometimes called the "Osirian" Resurrection. In the version of the story that was popular in Ancient Heliopolis, Geb and Nut symbolized the Earth and the sky respectively. Geb and Nut gave birth to two pair of twins – Set and Nephthys and the other pair was Ausar and Auset. Ausar is known to many people as "Osiris" and Auset is known to many as "Isis" - their offspring, Heru, is known as "Horus". "Osiris", "Isis", and "Horus" are Greek corruptions of their original names. Ausar assumed the position of king. What Ausar symbolized is our great potential for mastery. The crook and the flail that he is often presented with symbolizes his aptitude in husbandry including the farming of both plants and animals.

According to Kemetic folklore Ausar traveled around the world teaching the sciences and civilization to the uncivilized. His brother Set, who symbolizes the "lower self", was envious of Ausar. He invited Ausar to a banquet, and offered a prize for the person whose

---

[16]The word that the Kemites had for their language was Medu Neter. The "t" sound on the end of words in Medu Neter often represent femininity.

body fits perfectly within a particular chest. He had already secretly taken Ausar's measurements and he knew that he would fit perfectly into that chest. Once Ausur got into that chest, Set and his henchmen overtook Ausar, permanently closing this chest and dumped it into the Nile. It flowed down the Nile River. When that chest was finally found it was in the Middle East, in Syria.

Auset, Ausur's consort, took it upon herself to find this chest and this says a lot about what they thought of the female role in society. She succeeded in finding this chest, explained the situation to the Syrian king. She was able to acquire the body however Set got wind of it and took the body from Auset. Set then cut Ausar's body into fourteen different pieces. Set distributed body parts to several different places throughout the Nile Valley. However Auset was determined, loyal, and focused. She found all but one part, which was his phallus that was eaten by catfish. She put those pieces of his body back together and fashioned a phallus. Her straddling of Ausar resulted in the birth of Heru. In contrast to the biblical story of Eve, Pandora of Greek mythology, and the Northern Cradle culture in general, she is cast as a determined ally of Ausar, not the cause of his strife. Additionally, this story is the first Immaculate Conception story ever in human history and also the first resurrection story ever. This myth has been borrowed by several religious groups but aspects of it changed in other religions to fit particular cultural norms.

Kemetic spiritual concepts have influenced many religions, particularly Christianity, Islam, and Judaism. The borrowings become very clear when the

Image of the Auset (Isis) and Ausar on temple wall in Egypt.

Kemetic writings are compared with various scriptures. For example "The Book of Knowing the Creations", which was written millennia before the Bible, has a number of significant similarities with Bible mythology. "The Book of Knowing the Creations" states that:

> It is Ptah the Most Great who has given existence to all the divine powers and to their essences through his heart, mind, and tongue. Thus, it came to pass that the heart, mind, and tongue ruled all of the other members through teaching that Ptah is within everybody as heart and mind. And within every mouth as tongue all of the divine powers all of humankind, of cattle, all creeping things, and all living things. And He thinks as heart and mind and command as tongue wherever he wishes.
>
> Ptah's company of divine powers are before him in teeth and lips and are the teeth and lips which establishes the names of all things. And from which came forth Shu, the powers of light and air. And Tefnut, the power of moisture and brought into being the company of divine powers themselves...
>
> And thus, we made every work and all crafts, the actions of the arms and hands, the motions of the legs, the movement of every movement of the body, according to the command which is conceived by the heart and mind, brought forth by the tongue which creates the usefulness and

action of everything.

It is said of Ptah then, He is He who made all and created the divine powers, he is Ta-tenin, (the Risen Land) who produced the divine powers and from whom everything came forth, food and provisions, divine offerings and every good thing.

Thus, it was recognized and understood that he is the mightiest of all divine powers and after he had created all things and all the divine utterances, Ptah was pleased and rested.[17]

Let us compare this passage with the book of Genesis in the *King James Bible*:

In the beginning God created the heaven and the earth and the earth was without form and void and darkness was upon the face of the deep and the spirit of God moved upon the face of the waters and God said let there be light and there was light and God saw the light that it was good and God divided the light from darkness and God called the light day and the darkness he called light and the evening and the morning were the first day. And God said let there be firmament in the midst of the waters to divide the waters from the waters…God called the firmament heaven and the evening and the morning were the second day. And God said let

---

[17]Maulana Karenga, *Selections From the Husia: Sacred Wisdom of Ancient Egypt*, (Sankore Press: 1984), pg. 7

the waters under the heaven be gathered together unto one place and let the dry land appear and it was so. And God called the dry land earth and the gathering together of the water he called the sea and God saw that it was good...Thus the heavens and the earth were finished and all the host of them and on the seventh day God ended his work which he had made and he rested on the seventh day from all his work which he had made.

This is one of countless borrowings from the *King James Version* of *The Bible* that was taken from the Nile Valley conceptualization of creation.[18]

According to Egyptian mythology Set and Heru also had a clash. This conflict had important cultural implications. When Heru was a child his mother Auset had to hide Heru from Set. Throughout Kemet there are various images in stone of Auset hiding Heru in the papyrus bushes. As Heru matured to become a young man he fought with his uncle, Set. You can read a lot into the conflict between Heru and Set. It has been argued that this story suggests an issue of matrilineal versus the patrilineal way of life - and of course African societies practiced the matrilineal way of life. It is birth from the divine blood line that gives you the right to rule in the matrilineal system. This conclusion is acceptable on one level however the significance is multi-layered. One a deeper level it represents the uniting of the higher and lower self.Heru symbolizes

---

[18] The literature on this topic is vast. For starters see John G. Jackson's *Christianity Before Christ* and Acharya S's *The Christ Conspiracy: The Greatest Story Ever Sold.*

the higher self, and Set symbolizes the more self-centered lower self. However this instinct is necessary and is only destructive when it is corrupted or perverted. For example, our desire to procreate is innate and divine. However when it becomes perverted, issues of hyper-sexuality or confused sexuality arise. Also, our drive to be self-acknowledged, to understand our own power, our own divinity is innate and divine. However when it becomes perverted the ego overtakes reason – this affliction clouds the judgment. This imbalance is harmful not only to the individual but to humanity in general. The balanced individual with balanced "Heru" and "Set" instincts will be in tune with MA'AT.

(Luxor Temple) This carving of Heru and Set is a metaphor for the concept of Sema Tawi. The literal translation of Sema Tawi is "Union of the Two Lands". The deeper meaning is the union of the higher and the lower self.

Above is the Pyramid of Unas, a 5th Dynasty king. The Forty-Two Declarations of Innocence were first found inside this pyramid.

This "Judgment Scene" is from an artifact called the Papyrus of Hunefer.

The Kemetic temple of *Ipet Resyt*, is commonly referred to today as the temple of Luxor. This temple and the Karnak Temple were the universities of the day. Kemetic priests were the most knowledgeable community in the world until well after the collapse of Ancient Egypt. They lived a highly disciplined life and provided ethical guidance for the society as a whole.

MA'AT and the Forty Two Declarations of Innocence

The various Kemetic nomes were partial to particular stories that relate to the creation of humanity. Though the Neteru in these stories were mostly the same, the stories were somewhat different.   But what is consistent is the whole concept of MA'AT.   MA'AT and "The Forty Two Declarations of Innocence" became known to us in the modern world by way of the pyramid of Unas in Memphis.   MA'AT was the guiding principle of Nile Valley life and thought. MA'AT encompassed *truth, order, justice, righteousness, harmony, reciprocity*.

Another of the key sources that gives insight into the Kemetic spiritual concept is the *Pert Em Heru* – which literally means the "Book of Coming Forth By Day". This text was typically buried with royalty or the priesthood – it consists of words of power to steer the soul to the afterlife. Europeans refer to it as the "book of the dead" because it was buried with the "dead". The "Judgment Scene" on the previous page is taken from the *Pert Em Heru/Book of Coming Forth by Day* of a New Kingdom scribe by the name of Hunefer. Hunefer is led by Anubis (the jackal-headed deity of the underworld) to the hall of MA'ATI and seven neteru say yes to Hunefer's entrance by the showing of the Ankh while seven "vote" no. Failure to enter the halls of MA'ATI resulted in the loss of existence for the soul in contrast to the western concept of eternal hellfire. The heart is then balanced on the scale against the ostrich feather of MA'AT. The goal of every Kemite was to be in accord with MA'AT. If your actions were consistent with the virtues of MA'AT then your heart, on the left scale, would not be heavier than that ostrich feather that is on the right scale. Atop the scale is MA'AT personified as a woman with a feather on her head. Recording the scene is Djehuti – the neter who personifies knowledge and wisdom. The depiction of "composite", or part animal/part human, deities is a reflection of the natural environment around them. Still today you will see the ibis bird whose beak inspires Djehuti's beak and his pen. Hunefer prevails, with his heart lighter than the feather of MA'AT, and is led by Heru into the halls of MA'ATI.

It is clear that the origins and orientation of the Kemites was southward. Additionally, it is clear that Ancient Egypt was a part of a larger Ancient Nile Valley cultural complex that began at one end of the Nile and had its greatest elaboration in the form of Kemet at the other end.

Suggested Readings

Muata Ashby, *Egyptian Yoga*. Ashby is a foremost scholar on the subject of Kemetic spirituality. This text gives excellent introductory information on the subject.

Jacob Carruthers, *Essays in Ancient Egyptian Studies*. This book offers a nicely written account of the Two Cradle Theory and the concept of MA'AT. Also read his other two books entitled *Mdw Ntr: Divine Speech* and *Intellectual Warfare*.

Charles Finch, *The Star of Deep Beginnings*. The focus of this book is science during Antiquity in continental Africa. It is a superb book.

Josef Ben-Jochannon, *Black Man of the Nile*. This book is densely packed with information on the Nile Valley and Carthage. Every ambitious student should read each page of this text.

Ivan Van Sertima, *Egypt Revisited*. This book is comprised of essays by several experienced researchers on Nile Valley History and culture. It is a fountain of information.

Robin Walker, *When We Ruled*. This text addresses in great depth many of the most important issues related to our history.

Ancient Egypt in Global Context

In the Fall of 2011 I had a humorous, yet inspiring experience. I attended a presentation by a very race-conscious Egyptologist by the name of Bob Brier. What made this lecture that much more intriguing is that it was given in a classroom at Texas Southern University, which is a HBCU and also my alma mater. Brier has stated on the record that he tells his Black students that they should look only to the 25th Dynasty for the presence of "their" ancestors in Kemet. Sparks started to fly when a student asked Brier if Napoleon shot the nose off the sphinx. Immediately Brier charged the student with asking "a Black question" and the classroom was in an uproar. Brier continued that such claims are incorrect and posited only by "Afrocentric" scholars. The problem that most Eurocentric scholars face is that many of their exhortations are only lies agreed upon and fail to hold up against the most basic logic. For example, Brier claimed this day that wind erosion was responsible for the missing nose. One half-interested student asked why such erosion had not occurred elsewhere. What ensued was the greatest backpedaling exhibition by Brier that I had ever seen in an academic environment. No clear answer was given.

Brier's impatience with curious undergraduate students is humorous on one level but quite telling when one looks just beneath the surface. The tower of lies built by westerners in regard to Ancient Egypt are thinly constructed and will certainly collapse in the 21st century under the pressure of well-reasoned arguments and evidence. A glance at the Sphinx will illustrate the tenuous nature of mainstream Egyptology.

The Kemites called the Sphinx *Her Em Akhet*, which means "Heru on the Horizon". Heru can be looked at a couple different ways. For one Heru is the offspring of Ausar and Auset, who many know as Osiris and Isis. The king/suten/pharaoh is recognized as Heru on Earth – in essence he is born divine. This relates to the "divine Kingship" concept that I addressed in the previous chapter. A broad analysis of Her Em Akhet yields fruitful conclusions. To begin with, it gives us some indication of the antiquity of Kemetic civilization or Nile Valley civilization as a whole. Unfortunately mainstream Egyptologists tend to toe the party line on this topic. Most of them accept and perpetuate the belief that the human face of the Sphinx was built to represent a 4th Dynasty king named Khafre. However it is much more likely that the sphinx was built before or between 10,000 BCE – 7,000 BCE.[1] As with so many other questions related to the African experience, important answers are revealed in the environmental history of the land. A good example is the vertical grooves going up and down Her Em Akhet. Up and down and all the way around the complex of this great monolith are indentations. It has become apparent that these grooves were created by the water that flowed downward on Her Em Ahket. Kemet was established circa 5500 BCE – a time period when this region received only a few inches of rainfall per year. Therefore the only logical conclusion is that Her Em

---

[1]For a more thorough introduction to this topic see Sebai Muata Ashby's *The Priests and Priestesses of Ancient Egypt* (Miami: Cruzian Mystic Books, 2004), pg. 13.

Akhet was sculpted before the establishment of Kemet. In fact, the most recent time period that there would have been sufficient enough rainfall to create the indentations was 10,000 BCE-7,000 BCE.

We can glean so much more from this knowledge of Her Em Akhet. For one, this suggests that the indigenous people of that region had the artisanal skills to build sophisticated structures in stone before Narmer united the two lands. Secondly, it reveals that the spiritual concepts and mythology existed before the two lands merged. Lastly and what I would consider to be most important, is that this construction suggests that the indigenous people of that land were capable of organizing themselves for large-scale endeavors before the two lands united.

The Reign of Pepe II

As I stated in the previous chapter, the Kemetic "Kingdoms" were typified by sustained peace. During these periods folks generally got along with their neighbors, paid taxes, and worked together to build great achievements. Again, these three periods of stability are the Old Kingdom, the Middle Kingdom, and the New Kingdom. Between the periods of stability were two periods of great instability called "Intermediate" periods. During these periods communities were unstable, people were not working together, and neighbors were distrustful of each other. The very last king of the First Kingdom was a king named Neter Ka Ra Pepi, commonly referred to as Pepi

Her Em Akhet, popularly known as the Sphinx.

Sculpture of Pepi II in the lap of his mother. This style emulates images of Heru in the lap of his mother Auset.

II. Let us see if we can approximate the meaning of his name. The word "nefer" means beauty, "ka" is that part of your soul that is of the universe, "Ra" means God/Creator. The approximate meaning of his name is "The Beauty of the Soul of God". Pepi II came to the kingship at a very young age (about six years old) and his period of rule was longer than any monarch in human history. He ruled for ninety-four years. One of Pepi II's actions gives us insight into how Kemites looked at themselves in the context of the whole of Africa. When he was six years old he had a vizier named Harkuf. A vizier is akin to a prime minister and Harkuf carried out responsibilities on behalf of Pepi. Harkuf took expeditions to various parts of Africa. On one occasion he asked Harkouf to bring back to him a Twa. You may not have heard the word Twa before, but you have probably heard the term "pigmy". The Twa do not refer to themselves as pigmies, Europeans gave them that name and the term pigmy is quite pejorative. The proper name for this diminutive population of central Africa is Twa. Why would Pepi ask for a Twa? It is because of who the Twa symbolized to the Kemite's. One of the Kemites' oldest deities is called Bes. Bes is represented with the stature of a Twa. The Kemites saw a relationship between themselves and the Twa are amongst the world's oldest people.

Ancient Nile Valley Writing Systems

During this Golden Age in African History, writing was not only on paper but also etched in stone. Writings were done in stone with the expectation that they would last longer than what was written on paper. Kemites used three types of writing. The first is called *Medu Neter* or "divine speech". The writings on stone are usually written in Medu Neter. It is the oldest writing form that you will find in Kemet. Greeks called this writing system hieroglyphics, which means "sacred carvings" in Greek. A second form of writing was called *Hieratic*, which is akin to writing in cursive. Keep in mind that this is the same language just written

Medu Neter   **Hieratic**   **Demotic**

in different "scripts". Hieratic became much more common in the latter years of the Old Kingdom. And the reason they wrote in Hieratic as opposed to Medtu Neter was because this cursive writing was written more quickly. The third script is called Demotic. Demotic become common during the New Kingdom. Most of what we know about personalities or about medicine comes from one of these three scripts.

It was not until 1822 that the Medu Neter, which is the best known of these three scripts, was actually deciphered. This means that Jean-Francois Champollion, who was credited with deciphering it,

The Rosetta Stone – created about 196 B.C.E. and deciphered by Jean-Francois Champollion in 1822. The script at the top of the stone is Medu Neter, the script in the middle is Demotic, and the script at the bottom is Greek.

Medtu Neter
"writing the divine words,"

Deciphering Medu Neter

Medu Neter is read from the direction that the animals and people are facing. If the animals and people are facing the left then you begin on the left and move towards the right. This writing system has *ideographic* symbols and *phonetic* symbols. Phonetic means that the symbols are all used to make a sound. For example the loaf of bread is used to make the "t" sound. The hand is used to make the "d" sound. The chickling is used to make the "hu" sound. The staff is an ideograph for Medtu, which is translated into "speech". The symbol next to it is an ideograph for Neter, which translates as "divinity". The lines to the far right is a classifier. This symbol clarifies that we are speaking in the plural. The phrase translates into "writing the divine words".

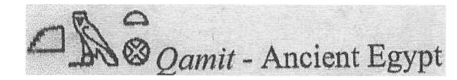

Kemet Written In Medu Neter

The charred wood to the far left means black or blackness. Its sound is "km" or "qam". Next the owl is the phonetic sound "m". The loaf of bread is used to make the "t" sound. At the bottom right is a crossroads. This determinative clarifies that we are speaking about a state or urban center. Sometimes it seems as though it's used to mean an urban center and sometimes it's used to mean a state or state power. However we know that the combination of symbols means Kemet and what ensures that we know that is the crossroads as a determinative.

The Shenu (sometimes called "cartouche")

The encirclement above is called a *shenu*. The shenu is a spiritual tool. It is a protector for the individual whose name is written inside the shenu. Due to the similarity of its shape to a bullet, Europeans began to call it a *cartouche*, which is the French word for bullet. The name inside the shenu is none other than Ramses II or Ramesu. The first symbol to the left means Ra. The dot inside the symbol for Ra is the creator of all things. In African cosmology, all things originate from the creator. This area between the dot and the larger circle symbolizes all things in existence – which emanate from Ra (the creator). The next symbol to the right of Ra is fox tails. The corresponding sound for the fox tails is "mes", which means "son of". Thus Ramesu means "son of God".

was able to transliterate the stone. This means he was able to figure out the symbols that correlated to the symbols in Demotic. You would have to be inundated in that culture to know the deeper understanding of language. Yet, the contribution of Champollion and other scholars enable us to have a fuller understanding of Kemetic cosmology.

Champollion transliterated a key word - which was "Ptolemy". He utilized his proficiency in Coptic to transliterate from Demotic to Greek. Coptic is essentially the language of Kemet written with Greek alphabets. Because of his facility with language, he was able to transliterate the Medtu Neter atop the stone. Henceforth the deciphering of Medu Neter was advanced by a number of researchers from various intellectual communities.

The First Intermediate Period

Studying the achievements of our ancestors is an endeavor that is fruitful beyond measure. In addition to celebrating our ancient achievements, we must study the circumstances that led to the demise of the great civilizations that our ancestors established. The greatest use of history is its use in predicting future outcomes. Thus, an analysis of the conditions that brought about the collapse of the Old Kingdom, the longest reigning regime in the history of government, is appropriate.

What were the conditions that led to this period of extreme instability and chaos? The First Intermediate Period emerged as the nomarchs began to challenge the power of the suten. Each nome, or region had a leader who was responsible to the suten. That leader was called a nomarch. Several of the nomarchs wanted more control, more power, and more physical/material benefits from their position. This tension was exacerbated by their interactions with foreigners to the north and migrations into Lower Kemet. Furthermore, these events transpired as competition for food resources intensified.

There are ancient writings in stone and papyri that convey the thoughts and feelings of the Kemites who lived throughout that time. "The Book of Ipuwer" is an ancient text that describes the sentiments of a Kemite during The First Intermediate Period. It is essentially a poem that was originally published during The Middle Kingdom. It is published in a compilation of ancient texts called *The Husia.*[2] The text states:

> The foreigners from without have come to Egypt and the Egyptian of yesterday cannot be found anywhere…Lo, the unrestrained says: 'If I knew where God is, I would serve Him'.[3]

These words bear a striking resemblance to contemporary times. Today there is mounting disappointment in mainstream religious leaders and the path of divinity is elusive. Consequently the communities that are in harmony with the universe can only be found in small pockets. The greatest shortcoming of humanity is that they have adopted

---

[2] In Medu Neter *hu-sia* translates into "authoritative utterance".
[3] "The Book of Ipuwer", translated by Maulana Karenga, *Selections from The Husia: Sacred Wisdom of Ancient Egypt*, (Los Angeles: University of Sankore Press, 1984), pg. 78-79.

foreign values that are essentially anti-earth and anti-life. This is the primary factor that disables us from acknowledging the divinity in all things, including humanity. Peace and stability is not the forte of the self-destructive.

Another valuable ancient text that was published in *The Husia* is the "The Book of Dialog With the Soul". There has probably been a moment in each person's life when they have had a dialog with the soul. Perhaps you have pondered to yourself, "Am I doing what is right"? "Will humanity come together to establish a more harmonious culture that is en suite with our original human ancestors?" Doubt loomed during The First Intermediate Period – as it does today. A passage from "the Dialog With The Soul" states:

> To whom shall I speak today? The one doing wrong is an intimate friend and the brother with whom one used to deal is an enemy. No one remembers the past and none return the good deed that is done. Brothers and sisters are evil and people turn to strangers for righteousness and affection.[4]

The fragmentation described above ultimately leads to distrust, poor resource management, instability. Today economic development is the mantra of many within our communities. Most of these talking heads focus on financially intelligence and individual financial success. However financial strength calls for cooperative action and cooperative economics. Failure

---

[4] "The Dialog With the Soul", ", translated by Maulana Karenga, *Selections from The Husia*, pg. 80-81.

in this area has created a dearth of financial and intellectual resources in our communities. A perpetual result has been capital outflow, which a perfect recipe for perpetual impoverishment. The poem continues, "...Brothers and sisters are evil and people turn to strangers for righteousness and affection". This clearly expresses that the foundations of their society had eroded.

The Middle Kingdom and the Reestablishment of Kemet

One of the greatest benefits of studying the past is that you come to learn that change is inevitable and that outcomes can be conceived and created. Essential to this is the belief that your thoughts and spiritual activity can manifest in this earthly realm if backed by determined, well-conceived action. Wahankh Intef II of 11th dynasty was among those that applied these principles to bring the Kemites out of their period of instability. Throughout Kemetic history, kings from the upstream areas down south either united the two lands or doggedly moved things in that direction. This dynamic is exactly the same during the intermediate period. One of the central figures of the Intermediate Period was Intef II and he also emerged from the south. He reigned for forty nine years and expanded the territory under his rule, however he did not completely unite Upper and Lower Kemet. Intef II managed to strengthen the kingdom, allowing for the eventual Sema Tawi that ushered in The Middle Kingdom.

Funerary stele of Wahankh Intef II of the 11th Dynasty. Intef II emerged as a leader during The First Intermediate Period. He reigned for 49 years, increased the stability of the country, and expanded the territory of the kingdom.

**(At the Egyptian Museum at Cairo)
Nebhepetre Mentuhotep II. He ruled during The Middle Kingdom and reigned for 51 years.**

Nebhepetre Mentuhotep II completed the job and brought the two lands together. Mentuhotep II's ancestors stabilized a substantial region just south of Thebes extending all the way to the First Cataract. Mentuhotep II organized his forces to subdue his challengers in the northern region of Herakleopolis. His leadership resulted in the reemergence of a unified Kemet. Consider that there was an Intef the 1st, a Mentuhotep the 1st and a host of other ancestors who had the exact same charge and set the process in motion. However it was their offspring – Intef II and Mentuhotep II that completed the process of reestablishing Semi Tawi.

On the subject of their race and ethnicity – they were black people without any equivocation. He or she who controls your education controls your sub-conscious thinking as well. Nile Valley Civilization is the greatest cultural complex that has ever existed. The reality of their black African genetic and cultural origins is unsettling to victims of western socialization.

Kemetic Literature in the Middle Kingdom

As the resurrection ushered in the Middle Kingdom, the Kemites used literature to ensure that the people remembered their history and their cultural origins. Kemetic literature emphasized triumph over previous personal and national challenges. These points are illustrated by "The Book of Nerferti", which is a piece of Middle Kingdom literature. It is important to mention that this account makes reference to a real life Kemetic king of the early Old Kingdom:

"And his majesty Pharoah Snefru said: 'Come Neferti, my friend and speak to me some beautiful words and well-chosen phrases which might please me upon hearing them.' And the teacher-priest, Neferti, deplored what had come to pass in Egypt, speaking on the condition of the East where Asiatic peoples roam in strength, frightening those about to harvest their crops and seizing cattle even at the plough. He said: Be moved my heart and mourn for this land in which you were born. For there is silence before evil; what should be condemned is feared and the great are overthrown in the land of birth. Tire not then while this evil exists. Rise up against that which is before you. For lo, the great no longer rule the land and what was established has now been undone. May Ra begin to re-establish this land... But a king shall come from the south named Ameni, the vindicated one, the son of a woman from Nubia.[5]

It is important to note that in the literature of this era commonly accepted the depiction of the barbaric "Asiatic" or the valorous southern hero that emerges from the highlands. He continues:

He will join together the Double Crown and the land will be enclosed in his grasp. The people of his reign will rejoice, for Ameni, the son of man,

---

[5] "The Book of Neferti", translated by Maulana Karenga, *Selections from The Husia*, pg. 85-87.

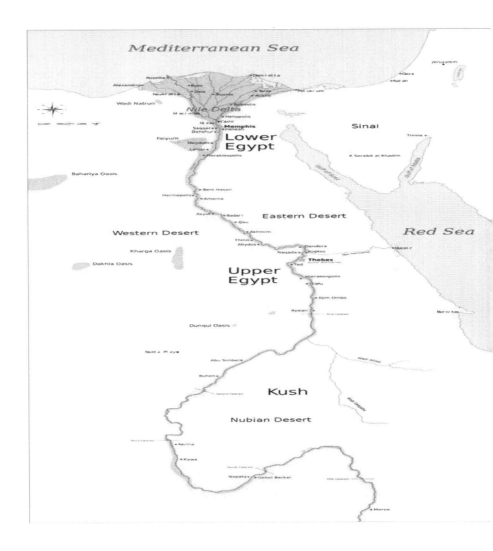

Intef and Menuhotep came from the south. This is a recurring theme in Kemet. Narmer, who united the two lands came from upstream (the south). Also, the leaders that brought about the New Kingdom emerged from the southern stretches.

will make his name for all eternity. The evil-minded plotters of treason will hold back their speech through fear of him. The Asiatic *invaders* will be consumed by his flame. Rebels will yield before his wrath and traitors will be brought low by his might. Then MA'AT, righteousness and order, will return to its place and Isfet, evil and chaos, will be driven away".[6]

"The Book of Nerferti" exemplifies how literature and history were combined to reinforce Kemetic pride and allegiance. This objective is the very roots of the story-telling tradition.

Kemetic Medicine

The Smith Medical Papyrus relates to surgical methods used in Ancient Egyptians. The Ebers Papyrus addresses the treatment of various ailments with natural remedies. Kemetic healers used both psychic and physical remedies. Studies prove that healing is more likely to transpire once a patient believes that they have the capacity to heal. A number of experiments have proven that people who believe are more likely to be healed. Thus, remedies had spiritual as well as more apparent approaches.

Take for example a treatment from the Ebers papyrus for the disease of scurvy. Their remedy was the increased intake of onions. We know now that a deficiency of vitamin c causes scurvy in humans. A conservative estimate for the writing of the Ebers

---

[6] Ibid., pg. 87.

Payrus is about 1900 BCE - some 1000 years before the first piece of European literature appeared in the form of *The Iliad*. Another interesting remedy was the use of honey as a disinfectant of burns and infections. They surmised that honey in conjunction with naturally produced enzymes created hydrogen peroxide. It is safe to say that the fathers and mothers of medicine are the healers of ancient Nile Valley civilizations.

When we hear people say they – the Ancient Egyptians - practiced magic or that they used "spells" to help them get better, keep in mind that this belief is similar to the practice prayer that is used today. Furthermore, the remedies of Kemetic medicine illustrate that priests had extensive knowledge of physiology and science – and the willingness to blend "disciplines" to solve problems.[7]

Kemetic temples frequently had a *per-ankh*, "house of life", outside of their temples. Kemites practiced a medical system that we would call today socialized healthcare. In essence, if you were a Kemite you were going to be treated by the well-studied at the per-ankh. All sectors of Kemetic society were controlled by priests including the medical sector.

The Second Intermediate Period

Again, Kemet had very long periods of stability and relatively short periods of chaos/instability. The Second Intermediate period tells us more about the causes of

---

[7] See a translated version of either the Ebers or Smith Papyrus. Also see Charles Finch's *The African Background to Medical Science*, Karnak House, 1990.

The Edwin Smith Surgical Papyrus (above). Smith was a German.

The Ebers Medical Papyrus. Ebers was an American.

instability than the First Intermediate Period. Just as during the First Intermediate Period, there was a power imbalance of power between the nomarchs and the king/suten. The king was unable to sustain total authority of nomes in Lower Kemet. What was it about Lower Kemet and why did this problem arise *again* in that area? For one, the seat of power for the Kemetic throne was moved to the town of *Waset*, which is today known as Luxor. Thus, it was moved further upstream – a greater distance from the root of the problem in Lower Kemet. The disconnect between the nomarchs and sutens, combined with the relative freedom in which the nomarchs had to operate set the stage for the chaos that emerged.

Another factor that created discord was the mounting influence of outsiders. Consistently, throughout the course of history – whether in Antiquity or recent times – outsiders have lined up to exploit the fragmentation of black communities. This was the case during Kemet's Second Intermediate Period. On this occasion it was the Semitic Hyksos - from the Northern Cradle.

As expressed earlier the worldview of the Northern Cradle cultures is completely incompatible with the worldview of indigenous African cultures in general and Kemetic culture in particular. As this mutated "European" and "Asian" emerged in the southern stretches around 4,000 BCE, the lands we know as India, Saudi Arabia, and the Tigris/Euphrates were inhabited by Africans that emerged from the Southern Cradle. The humanistic, Southern Cradle cultures were predicated on the idea that humanity must be in harmony with the universe, self-sufficiency, and respectful of contributions of male and female members of society. The Hyksos "invasion" began by way of infiltration - as has been the norm in the colonization of African societies. By the 12th Dynasty Hyksos claimed the throne of Kemet.

It is clear that Kemetic royalty never submitted to Hyksos rule and fought for generations to return the throne to their African bloodlines. During this second intermediate period Kemetic freedom fighters sought refuge in the highlands and organized themselves for resumption of their rightful place. By the time of Sequenenre Tao II, the last king of 17th Dynasty, the effort to restore MA'AT to the lands was underway.

Contact between the two cultures began to occur as the Hyksos established themselves at Avares, in the eastern part of the delta. Avares became an administrative center during the time of the Hyksos' rule.

(Above) From the tomb of Khnumhotep at Beni Hassan, an image of the Hyksos' (shepherd kings) immigration to Kemet. Here they come with animal life, suggestive of a pastoralist past, and the compound bow that they introduced into Kemet.

Seqenenre Tao II was among the first leaders to lead armed campaigns against the Hyksos to reclaim the throne. Note the axe marks on the skull - he died in battle.

Above is the axe of Ahmose, which was buried with Queen Aahotep. Queen Aahotep lived to be one hundred years old. In the middle of the axe is *smiting,* which is when the final blow is delivered to a prostrated enemy. It was common to depict kings that were successful in battle in the smiting position.

Queen Aahotep and the Warrior Spirit

Queen Aahotep's actions reflect the warrior spirit that was necessary to defeat the Hyksos. She was the great wife of Seqenenre Tao II and the mother of both Kamose and Ahmose. After the death of Seqenenre Tao II and his son Kamose who likely died during this war of liberation, Queen Aahotep was the sole guardian of their child Ahmose. She maintained the war effort against the Hyksos. A stele found at Karnak Temple reads:

> The king's wife, the noble lady, who knew everything assembled Kemet. She looked after what her sovereign had established. She guarded it. She assembled her fugitives. She

brought together her deserters. She pacified her
Upper Egyptians. She subdued her rebels.
The king's wife Ahotep given life.[8]

Aahotep served as regent until her son Ahmose
assumed kingship at seventeen years of age. Ahmose
had been socialized for this war and was highly
strategic in his war against the Hyksos. His application
of a three year blockade cut Avaris off from its Asiatic
ties. It was Ahmose who united the whole of Kemet
and also he began the military campaigns into Asia for
which Ramses II became so well known. Why the
campaigns in Asia? Ahmose must have realized that
they needed to stave off those Asian threats, such as the
Hyksos, who had been consistently migrating into
Africa. Ahmose' ascendency did not signal the end of
Aahotep's military influence. While Ahmose was away
on one of these campaigns it was his mother who
maintained order. On this occasion one of the nomarchs
began an insurrection, which Aahotep efficiently
suppressed. As a result of this service to the country,
she received the Golden Fly Award, which was one of
the highest awards given for service in battle. While
Ahmose is recognized as bringing about the 18th
Dynasty, the best known of all the Kemetic dynasties, it
must be noted that his reign and achievements may not
have been possible had Aahotep not exhibited and
maintained the warrior spirit at crucial moments in
Kemetic history.

---

[8] Ashra and Merira Kwesi. *African Builders of Civilization* (1995).

Ahmose here on his chariot fighting against the Hyksos.

The18th Dynasty: The Best Known Dynasty of Kemet

A distinction has to be made between the *popular* kings of the 18th Dynasty and the *great* kings of this dynasty. For example Akenaten is certainly one of the most popularly kings. He is often credited with the creation of the first monotheistic religion. However Akhenaton was not particularly great. Akhenation's worship of Aton did not introduce the Kemites to monotheism. This was as much a political decision designed to challenge corrupt priests. Kemites had long since been monotheistic. Additionally his passivist approach to dealing with national threats was truly not in the spirit of *Sema Tawi*. He chose not to defend the borders of the country against aggressive enemies. King Tutankhamun is another popular, yet not particularly great king. The only reason why King Tut is discussed as he is today is because his tomb was found intact, which was good for European tomb raiders such as Howard Carter and there guides.

Among the great suten/king/pharoah's of the 18th Dynasty is Hatshepsut. Although a highly spiritual individual, Hatshepsut surely to manifested in this realm of existence. One interesting note about her is that she used the claim of being born by way of Immaculate Conception (via Amen) to legitimize her kingship. This notion is illustrated on the wall of her mortuary temple at Deir el Bahri.

Hatshepsut strove to develop the economic infrastructure of Kemet by expanding the realm of trade. She revived the tradition of commercial expeditions by sending conveys northward for wood,

**King Khemt Amen Maat Ka Ra Hatshepsut
(daughter of Tutmose I)**

(Above) Hatshepsut's mortuary temple, *Zosret Zosru* (the most holiest and select of places). Depictions in this temple acknowledges her biological father (Thutmose I) and her spiritual father *Amen*. Hatshepsut felt an affinity for Mentuhotep II and her mortuary temple was built adjacent to his. The architectural style of her temple was influenced by Mentuhotep II's.

(above) The King's List at Abydos, Upper Egypt. The King's List is one of the oldest and most reliable historical documents in existence. It is dedicated to Seti I. The image above depicts Seti I presenting his ancestors to his son Ramses II. Inside each shenu is the name of the preceding kings from Narmer to Seti I. One of the ways we know the sequence of kings is by the kings list at Abydos.

(above) Seti I's Temple at Abydos.
A depiction of Seti I wearing the Kepresh (war helmet) while holding up MA'AT.

for turquoise and copper, and southward by way of the Red Sea for her famous Punt expedition for valuable spices. Although history does not depict her as particularly valorous, it bears mentioning that The Two Lands were never attacked or threatened during her rule. Furthermore, Hatshepsut revered the warrior king Mentuhotep II, whose temple influenced her own.

Seti I and the Socialization of Ramses II

The last king of the 18th Dynasty was a warrior and skilled administrator named Horemheb. Horemheb worked doggedly and wisely to restore the political and religious order that had been undermined by Akhenaton's decision to delegitimize the cult of Amen. From within his ranks he built a close knit circle on which he relied for both political and military matters. He also established a regular building and restoration program of temples. He was particularly impressed with a young soldier by the name of Ramessu. Ramessu soon became troop commander and eventually the vizier to Horemheb. Horemheb had no heir to the throne and he came to acknowledge Ramessu as the crown prince. Upon Horemheb's death, Ramessu became king/pharaoh/suten and thus began the 19th Dynasty. The ascendancy of Ramessu demonstrates one way that the kingship could be transferred to a new "dynasty".

Ramessu a.k.a. Ramses I had a son named Seti I who was named after Ramses' father named Seti, as it had been their custom to name the son after the grandfather. Seti I became co-regent to his father Ramses I and was particularly interested in returning Kemetic authority to regions that had fallen beyond their control. Seti I maintained the tradition of military campaigns beyond their borders and attention to important monuments at home. Seti built his mortuary temple at Abydos and fought against the Syrians and Hittites. Seti I's son, Ramses II, accompanied his father on several of these excursions along the Mediterranean.

Ramses II became the best known of all the Kemetic kings and was certainly among the greatest. One of his greatest achievements was the rebuilding of various temples and monuments from Nubia all the way to the mouth of the Nile. He enhanced the major temples of Karnak and Luxor, built the reknowned Ramesseum in Thebes, and constructed the impressive monuments to himself and is great wife Nefertari at Abu Simbel.

Ramses II's military exploits are legendary. He was determined to subdue Kemet's enemies and continued the war efforts of the preceding 19th Dynasty kings. Ramses II moved his capital from Thebes to a town he built called Pi-Ramessu. Pi-Ramessu was built at Avaris, the location that was the seat of Hyksos power. This brought him into closer proximity of the regions that threatened his rule. He is acknowledged as having won more battles than any other Kemetic king.

What stands out among the Kemites, and the 19th Dynasty kings in particular, is their ardent spirituality. As seen in the previous image from Seti I's temple at Abydos, Seti I is depicted going into battle with MA'AT in his hand. This symbolizes that Seti I's military campaigns are in the name of righteousness. This spiritual focus is also exemplified by the account of Ramses II's military exploits at the Battle of Kadesh, which was written on several temple walls including

Karnak and Luxor. Popularly known as "The Poem of Pentaur", this work of literature provides a historical account of Ramses II's valor in battle at Kadesh in Syria. Furthermore it illustrates his faith in the almighty Amen Ra. Ramses went on this expedition with four squadrons – each named after a different deity (Set, Ptah, Ra, and Amen). Ramses II was ambushed with only his Amen division to deploy. Against what appeared to be insurmountable odds most of his troops abandoned him. Here I will quote the poem at length so that the reader can better understand Ramses II's worldview. In the midst of this melee Ramses II stated:

> "Yea, and not one of my princes, of my chief men
> and my great,
> Was with me, not a captain, not a knight;
> For my warriors and chariots had left me to my fate,
> Not one was there to take his part in fight."...
> "Father Ammon, where are you?
> Shall a sire forget his son?...
> Have I e'er transgressed your word?
> Disobeyed, or broke a vow?...
> ...to you I dedicated noble monuments, and filled
> Your temples with the prisoners of war?
> That for you a thousand years shall stand the shrines
> I dared to build?...
> Here I stand,
> All alone;
> There is no one at my side,
> My warriors and chariots afeared,
> Have deserted me, none heard
> My voice...
> But I find that Ammon's grace
> Is better far to me
> Than a million fighting men and ten thousand

chariots be….
To you my cry I send,
Unto earth's extremest end…
Ammon heard it, and he came unto my call;
And for joy I gave a shout,
From behind, his voice cried out,
"I have hastened to you, Ramses Miamun,
Behold! I stand with you,
Behold! 'tis I am he,
Own father thine, the great god Ra, the sun…."
Then all this came to pass, I was changed in my heart
Like Monthu, god of war, was I made,
With my left hand hurled the dart,
With my right I swung the blade…
like Monthu in his might,
I rushed on them apace,
And I let them taste my hand
In a twinkling moment's space.
Then cried one unto his mate,
"This is no man, this is he,
This is Sutek, god of hate"…
Then I lifted up my voice, and I spake,
"Ho! my warriors, charioteers,
Away with craven fears,
Halt, stand, and courage take,
Behold I am alone,
Yet Ammon is my helper, and his hand is with me
now."
These godless men are wretches that in Ammon put
no trust…
And I killed them, none escaped me, and I slew, and
slew, and slew…[9]

---

[9] "The Poem of Pentaur",.
http://www.reshafim.org.il/ad/egypt/kadeshaccounts.htm

(above) Temple to Ramses II at Abu Simbel. Ramses II's full name is User Maat Ra Setep En Ra Ramessu Meriamen. "User" means you are in control, you have dominion. "Maat Ra" roughly translates into "justice". "Setep En Ra means "chosen by God". Ramessu means "son of God". Meriamen means "beloved by Amen" or "beloved by God".

(above) The Temple of Luxor

The tall, erect structure in the front of the temple is called a tekhen – today it is often referred to as an obelisk. Due to westerners and their Egyptian allies, there are more Tehkenu outside of Kemet than there are inside of Kemet. The temples at Luxor and Karnak were like universities. Various disciplines were learned however spirituality and ethics were not excluded. An initiate would have learned the necessity of living in accord with MA'AT.

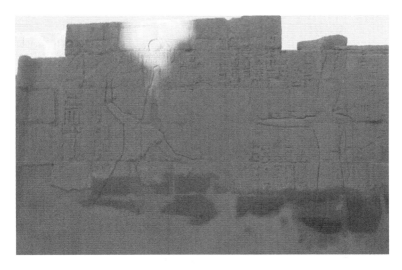

Ramses portraying himself in the smiting position. Since the days of King Narmer, who united the two lands, other kings have featured themselves smiting enemies. Ramses II's military exploits took him beyond the borders of Kemet however Ramses II was not a conqueror per se. Ramses' military actions beyond the borders of Kemet were proactive approaches to protecting Kemet.

Thus no sphere of Kemetic life was to succeed without the blessings of God, the neteru, and the ancestors.

Ramses II had several wives, the best known of which is Queen Nefertari, to whom he dedicated a temple adjacent to his own in Abu Simbel. He fathered over a hundred children and outlived most of them. He ruled for over sixty years. His namesake, Ramses III, of the subsequent 20th Dynasty was a formidable warrior as well.

The 25th Dynasty: More Saviors From the South

Consistently throughout the history of Kemet leadership arose from the southern stretches during periods of instability. This dynamic resulted in the establishment of the 25th Dynasty, which emerged from the Nubian region of Napata. The initial leader of this dynasty was Piankhy. Piankhy sustained the centuries-long battle with the Assyrians and campaigned beyond the borders of Africa as did the kings of the New Kingdom. The kings of the 25th Dynasty sought to preserve the indigenous Nile Valley. For example, Shabaka, the successor to Piankhy, had a papyrus that was found in Memphis (Lower Egypt) written in stone. This "Shabaka Stone" provides us with an understanding of Memphite Theology that was described earlier in this text. Another of the 25th Dynasty kings, Taharqa, continued the building tradition along the Nile including a number of pyramids in Nubia. Once Taharqa was defeated by the Assyrian troops stationed north of Memphis, he fell back to Nubia. Egypt has been under foreign control ever since.

,

The Shabaka Stone

The Shabaka Stone gets its name from the 25th Dynasty king named Shabaka. He had the remains of an Old Kingdom papyrus etched in stone to ensure the survival of the ancient document, which was a window into the past of Kemet. It is currently in the British Museum.

What Caused Kemet's Decline?

Eventual collapse is inevitable for any super power. What made Kemet unique relative to nearly all the countries that have achieved such a position is that military might was not the primary strength of the country – it was balance. The Kemites were spiritually in tune with each other and the universe as a whole. As noted earlier, it was held together by a common belief in MA'AT. Acquisition and application of knowledge, combined with good character were held in high esteem in Kemet. As the challenge of defending its borders became heightened, so did the militarization of the country – however militarization was not the sole source of its power. From the establishment of Kemet, beginning with King Narmer, to the collapse of the 25th Dynasty spanned a period of nearly 5,000 years. Throughout the course of this time Kemet was the leading country in the world.

To gain a fuller appreciation for the length of time which Egypt sustained itself as the premier country in the world, let us contrast Kemet with the prowess of the well-known European powers that came to power by war and plunder. Ancient Greece came into existence circa 8th Century B.C.E. and lasted to about the 6th Century C.E. throughout the whole existence of Greece it was not the premier power in the world. The same can be said of Ancient Rome. Ancient Rome came into existence about the 8th Century B.C.E. and collapsed about the 2nd Century C.E. The European powers of the "Modern" Era of history were preoccupied with "empire". The tenure of each as the premier power of the western world was extremely short relative to that of Ancient Egypt. Portugal's tenure as the dominant western power lasted less than one hundred years. Spain was the most formidable of the western powers for less than 200 years and that was only due to the acquisition of gold and forced labor in the Americas. Holland was the foremost western power for one hundred years or so from about 1700 to about 1800. England, perhaps the most successful of the European powers in the Modern Era, dominated the world politics and economics from about 1700 or so to about 1920. The United States was a dominant economic power going into the 20th century but the United States did not become a dominant political power until after World War I. In less than one hundred years since that time the United States is already experiencing an apparent decline. The strength of any institution is determined by the nature of its foundation. The foundation of Kemet was built on MA'AT, which emphasized harmony. The concept of harmony between humans and within the universe is what enabled humanity itself to become a successful species. Thus the European powers reign was short-lived because each was based on graft and murder – what the Kemites would have described as Isfet (Isfet is akin to chaos, the opposite of MA'AT).

In the case of Ancient Egypt it must be remembered that nothing can last forever. However there are some factors that I believe hastened the collapse of Kemet. The nature of their interaction with foreigners created the most destructive issues. This had been a problem since the days of Narmer. In fact the Narmer Palette reveals the vanquishing of foreigners was necessary for Narmer to consolidate his control over both regions. The immigration of the Asiatic Hyksos led to instability in the country, leading to the Second Intermediate Period. Throughout the New Kingdom Ancient Egypt was consistently threatened by foreigners including Libyans, Assyrians, and Hittites. Wars were fought on several fronts. During the reign of Ramses III the borders of Kemet was directly attacked by Libyans and their allies. Imagine the differences between the world of the early Old Kingdom, with the expenditure of excess energy and capital concentrated on architectural wonders that would stand the test of time. Consider the sophisticated medical and philosophical writings of the Old Kingdom by priests such as Imhotep and Ptahhotep. By the time of the 19th and 20th Dynasties kings attempted to employ spiritual technology by appealing to the Almighty and far less to the *neteru*. Furthermore they had to contend with corruption of priests and officials on a scale much greater than the Old Kingdom.

In an effort to diminish external pressures, alliances were affirmed with the marriage of Kemetic kings to foreign wives. This was a unidirectional phenomena since Kemetic kings did not send daughters or any royalty abroad as wives. This meant that the values of foreigners were consistently being interwoven with the traditional African/Kemetic worldview by matriarchs and their royal offspring. It also bears mentioning that Aton, the deity of Ankhenaton, may well have been imported to Kemet from abroad.

By the time of the 20th Dynasty economic stagnation and decline created problems for Kemet, combined with the encroachment of a dessert that had been expanding for several thousand years. The economic and environmental factors became even more pronounced as the population grew by way of natural growth and immigration. After over 5,000 years of accommodating increased numbers, the encroachments of foreigners, and the ever expanding Sahara, Kemet yielded to covetous foreigners from the Northern Cradle.

Stolen Legacy

The legacy of Kemet has been stolen by foreigners in more ways than one. The first is the notion that Greeks originated and authored what we know as Greek philosophy. It is well-known that Ancient Egyptian cosmology spread throughout the Mediterranean world. By the last millennium B.C.E. it had become common place for outsiders to seek the knowledge and wisdom of the Egyptians. The colonization of Alexandria (in the delta) by the Persians in 542 B.C.E. afforded several inhabitants, including Persians, Ionians and several other Mediterranean peoples, the chance to study at Alexandria. The opportunity to study directly with Egyptian priests was seized with great enthusiasm. Thales, who supposedly was the first to teach what is commonly accepted as Greek philosophy, came of age only after his studies in Kemet. Isocrates (436-338 B.C.E) said of the well-known Greek scholar Pythagoras that "He [Pythagoras] came to Egypt, and became the disciple of the people there; he was the first to bring philosophy to Greece." [10] Although several

---

[10] George G.M. James, *Stolen Legacy*, (originally published 1954; rpt. Houston: African Diaspora Press, 2012) pg.

(Left) The tekhen (also known as an obelisk by westerners) that was initially stolen away from Heliopolis by the Romans in the 1st Century BCE and taken to Alexandria. It was eventually stolen by the United States in 1881. It has stood in Central Park in New York City since.

(Right) This tekhen was stolen away from the Luxor Temple in Luxor, Egypt and has been in Paris, France since 1826.

Tekhenu are spiritual symbols that are metaphors for the resurrection of Ausar.

scholars of antiquity consistently credited the Ancient Egyptians as originators of higher knowledge, more recent scholars are largely responsible for the notion that Greek philosophy emerged from Greece without the template of Ancient Egyptian cosmology. This is one way that he legacy of Kemet was stolen.

The legacy of Kemet has also been stolen by the removal of sacred symbols and artifacts from the country of Egypt. To get an idea of the splender of Kemet one needs only to visit any of the museums in major cities throughout the world such as the Metropolitan Museum and the Brooklyn Museum in New York City. Included in that lot would be the British Museum in London and the Louvre in Paris. In thousands of the private and public museums throughout the world, you will find booty in the form of artifacts that were stolen and supposedly "gifted" by "Egyptians" who bear no cultural or genetic relationship with the Kemites. One example is the tekhenu (commonly referred to as obelisks by westerners) that are located in New York City, London, and Paris. The tekhenu that are in New York City and London were built by Tutmose III in the city Heliopolis. The tekhen (*u* is added to the end to denote plurality) in Paris is from the Luxor Temple in what is today Luxor, Egypt. The physical symbology of the tekhen is that of Ausar's phallus, which serves as a metaphor for the resurrection of Ausar. These sacred symbols were stolen from Egypt.

There are symbolizes all around you everywhere you go symbolizes of the greatness of ancient Kemet. and of Africa in general but if you are not trained to see it you never will and you'll be lost in a Eurocentric paradigm. A major step to understanding this arcane knowledge is to visit local museums in your area and also to visit the sacred tombs and temples of Kemet.

Suggested Readings

Michael Bradley. *The Iceman Inheritance: Prehistoric Sources of the Western Man's Racism, Sexism and Aggression* (1978)

This book gives excellent insight into the cultural divergence of Europeans away from human culture in general.

Anthony Browder. *Nile Valley Contributions to Civilization* (1992).

This book is a wonderful general account of Ancient Egypt. It addresses a range of important topics.

Charles S. Finch. *The African Background to Medical Science* (1990)

This unique text delves into the medical profession in Kemet and other traditional African societies. It dedicates a complete chapter to the great master Imhotep.

Drusilla Dunjee Houston. *Wonderful Ethiopians of the Ancient Cushite Empire* (1926)

This book uses various methodologies to explain the emergence of African/human culture. She is among the first scholars since Antiquity to address Kemet's Ethiopian origins. This book is a literary masterpiece that should be read by everyone.

George G.M. James. *Stolen Legacy* (1954)

This book provides an account of Ancient Egypt's philosophical influence on "Greek" philosophy. It provides a window into the Ancient Egpyptian Mystery School teachings. It also historicizes the Greeks' travels to Egypt and the Egyptian concepts they claimed.

Ashra and Merira Kwesi. *African Builders of Civilization* (1995).

This book is a compilation of biographies and pictures of Kemet's most influential historical figures. These brief sketches provide rare information based on decades of field study.

Dr. Perry Khepera Kyles

Presents

The Ancient Egypt "Sacred Lands" Tour

August 4-16, 2014

$ 3,500 – All Inclusive

Above: Dr Kyles at The Giza Plateau featuring the
Great   Pyramid.

The all-inclusive trip includes:

- round trip air fare from New York to Cairo
- deluxe hotel accommodations
- breakfast and dinner every day (lunch on five days)
- entrance into all monuments and temples
- presentations by Dr. Kyles at the hotels and the monuments
- boat rides, party at Nubian Village, and much more.

For information or an application please contact Dr.
Kyles at 832-322-4032 or e-mail at
professorkyles@yahoo.com

Made in the USA
San Bernardino, CA
10 June 2014